T0163046

The Spiritual Roots of the Holy Land

LAITMAN
KABBALAH
PUBLISHERS

The Spiritual Roots of the Holy Land

Published by Laitman Kabbalah Publishers
www.kabbalah.info info@kabbalah.info
1057 Steeles Avenue West, Suite 532, Toronto, ON, M2R 3X1, Canada
2009 85th Street #51, Brooklyn, New York, 11214, USA

Printed in Canada

ISBN 978-1-897448-66-3
Library of Congress Control Number: 2011933652

Translation: Irina Rudnev, Chaim Ratz
Copy Editor: Claire Gerus
Cover and Layout Design: David Gurovich
Executive Editor: Oleg Itsekson
Publishing and Post Production: Uri Laitman

FIRST EDITION: MARCH 2012
First printing

Contents

The International Kabbalah Education and Research Institute invites you to a fascinating journey to the spiritual roots of the Land of Israel. We'll trace the history of the wisdom of Kabbalah back to its birth, see where it began and how it progressed through the ages, and discover why this tiny patch of land never ceases to be the center of global attention.

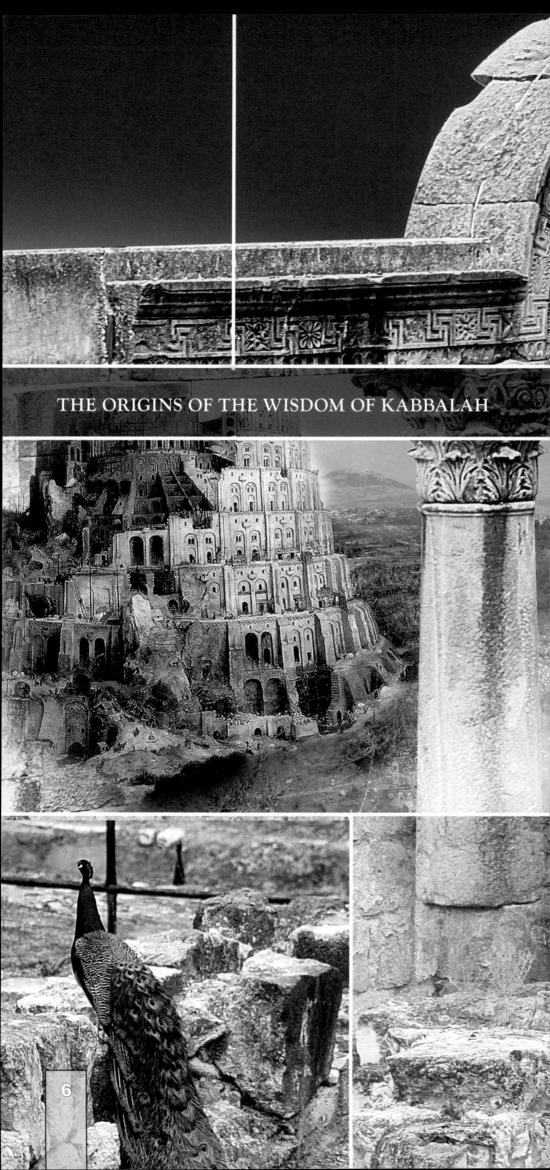

THE ORIGINS OF THE WISDOM OF KABBALAH

Our story begins some four thousand years ago in ancient Babylon, the cradle of modern civilization. Babylon was located in the fertile crescent known as Mesopotamia, and became a melting pot of peoples and cultures who lived in harmony, peace, and brotherhood.

But then a shift began: people started thinking only of themselves, and the feelings of brotherhood were crushed and trampled. This was the first time in history that the human ego had burst out of control, and the Babylonian harmony was shattered into pieces in what we now know as The Fall of the Tower of Babel. This was also the first time that humanity faced a choice—build a tower of selfish whims that would soon collapse, or follow the path to spiritual transcendence.

Mediterranean Sea

Israel

8

The man who offered the latter option to the Babylonians was a resident of Ur of the Chaldeans named Abraham, the son of Terach. Not long before Abraham had made that offer, he was still an idol worshipper, selling statuettes for a living. But Abraham wanted to understand what had happened to his people, so he began to search the nature of Creation for answers. In his search, he discovered that the ego did not swell in order to separate people. Rather, it was to invoke them to unite even more than before, and thus discover the superior force that creates all things. Indeed, Abraham's discovery came just when the world needed it, and he began to spread the word. In time, Abraham's students formed a group of Kabbalists and set out toward the land of Canaan, which would later become "the land of Israel."

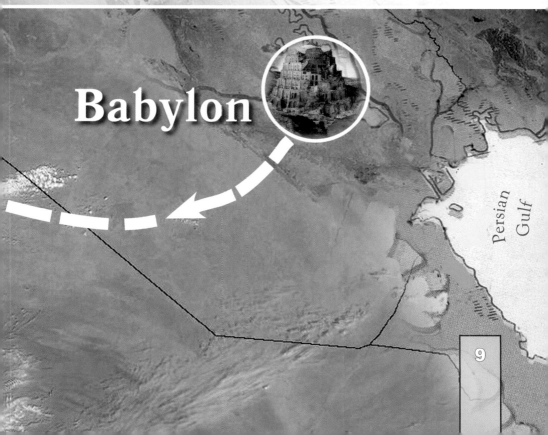

Babylon

Persian Gulf

WHY DID ABRAHAM LEAVE
FOR THE LAND OF ISRAEL?

When Abraham perceived the spiritual essence, the cause of all that was happening around him, he discovered that the manifestations and impact of the spiritual forces on our world were most evident in the land of Israel; this is why he brought his students there. This is also the reason why this land is regarded as sacred to the Abrahamic religions (Judaism, Christianity, and Islam), and why people have such profound experiences in this land.

The diversity of this tiny piece of land is truly astounding. Each part of it projects a unique spiritual quality, and each region invokes different sensations and experiences. Kabbalists tell us that it is from here that the spiritual forces spring forth and flow out to the rest of the world.

THE FORCES THAT AFFECT THE LAND OF ISRAEL DIVIDE IT INTO A NUMBER OF PARTS

Zeir Anpin

Five different forces—five *Sefirot*—affect the land of Israel: *Keter* (Crown), *Hochma* (Wisdom), *Bina* (Understanding), *Zeir Anpin* (Aramaic: Small Face), and *Malchut* (Kingship). The word *Sefira* (singular for *Sefirot*) comes from the word, "sapphire," which in Hebrew means "illuminating." *Sefirot* are spiritual qualities resembling "supernal roots," bearing a unique effect on each of the geographical areas of the land.

The five *Sefirot* are five levels of spiritual influence over our world, and the entire geography of the land of Israel is built according to those influences.

A Sefira (singular of Sefirot) is a spiritual quality that projects its influence on a specific part of the land of Israel.

15

270
Cableway
HAR DOV
2224
29.
999
KETEF HERMON
98
MAJDAL SHAMS
Newe-Ativ
Nimrod
989
W. Sa'ar
Ein Qiniyya
Mas'ada
Berekho

Zeir
Anpin

16

MOUNT HERMON (KETER)

The first and highest force, the onset of all that exists, the thought that will become an action, is called *Keter* (Crown). This is the force that affects Mount Hermon and its surroundings.

Keter is the highest spiritual quality, crowning the whole of Creation. This is the thought of Creation, which encompasses the creation of the world, the design of Creation's development, and its perfect future state.

Mount Hermon is the highest part of the land of Israel. Come winter, it is covered in "white-hair" made of snow.

20

Come summer, it is majestic, rock solid, and silent.

THE GALILEE
(HOCHMA)

The second spiritual force is called *Hochma* or "Wisdom." It is the embodiment of the thought, action, and Light without which life cannot be.

Hochma is the first stage of Creation, the "substance" from which the world is built. This is the Kli, the "vessel" in which the spiritual light shines forth.

The streams that flow down Mount Hermon and converge into the Jordan River symbolize the Light.

The waters that flow down the Golan Heights seep through the basalt rocks and the verdant valleys, then flow down the length of the Galilee.

The Kabbalists named the spiritual roots of these streams, "Thirty-Two Paths of Wisdom."

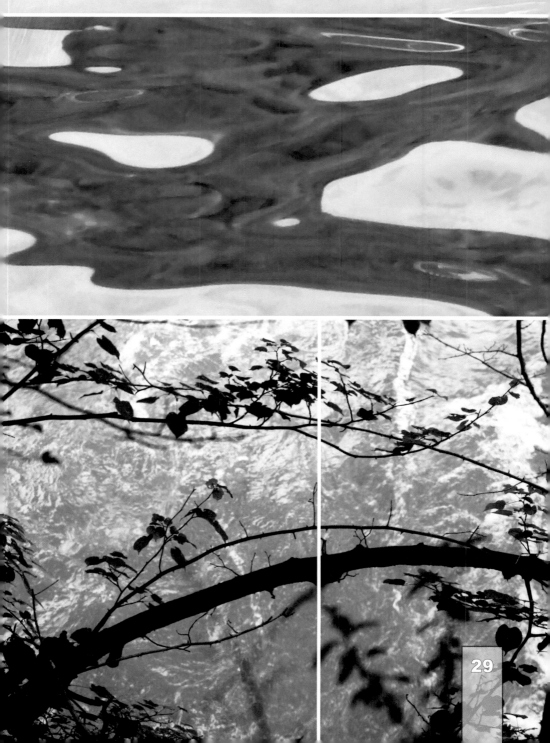

29

THE SEA OF GALILEE (YAM KINNERET) (BINA)

At the end of a long and winding journey, the streams of life-giving water flow into Yam Kinneret (known as "The Sea of Galilee," although it is really a lake). Yam Kinneret symbolizes the third spiritual force, *Bina* (Understanding), the foundation of unreserved giving that allows no selfish thought to be. *Bina* is a pure thought of the well-being of others.

Bina is a maternal quality, a pure and all-embracing love that shields us from the ego and directs us toward bestowal, toward giving.

32

Yam Kinneret is the water source that nourishes the whole of the land, filling its surroundings with its vital force and keeping nothing for itself.

Visitors from around the world come to the Kinneret. Here, one can almost touch the purity and peace.

THE HEART OF ISRAEL (ZEIR ANPIN)

Down the snowy heights of Mount Hermon, through the Galilee and the Kinneret, the waters flow on toward the Jordan Valley. This region aligns with the fourth spiritual force—*Zeir Anpin* (Small Face), which oversees movement and growth.

Zeir Anpin is the quality of growth, a force that brings life into the world, spiritually inseminating and nurturing it.

Springing from the three previous forces, the fourth one comes a step closer to our world and influences the area adjacent to Yam Kinneret, as well as the central part of the state, nourishing everything that is nurtured by *Bina*.

39

The waters of the Jordan River traverse the Kinneret, but do not blend with it. Instead, they flow on out and continue their journey southward. From a bird's-eye view, one can observe the resulting current in the water. In a similar way, *Hochma* (Wisdom) permeates the qualities of love and mercy, while never quite dissolving within them.

The agriculture in this area is highly developed, and the area is densely populated. This is also the location of the spiritual capital, Jerusalem—the very heart of the world, located precisely at the center of *Zeir Anpin*.

The Western Wall (also known as "The Wailing Wall") in Jerusalem is a place where people often pray or visit. It symbolizes the power to overcome human egoism.

According to the wisdom of Kabbalah, the only thing one should ever pray for is to be able to transcend one's ego. Aim for anything else, and the Wailing Wall becomes like any wall and the request will go unanswered.

Mār Sābā

N. Darga

JUDEA

Biq'at Hu...

Ḥar Herodyon
758

Teqoa

"Nature Reserve"

N. Teqoa

Avenat

ROSH TUR

Enot Qane

234

Enot Samar

Ma'ale-Amos

Mezoqe Deragot

Mizpe-Shalem

Yukh

"Nature Reserve"

557

N. Ḥazezon

Naḥal Arugot

624

Tim

425

MIZPE-QEDEM

YAM HA-MELAḤ (DEAD SEA)

En-Gedi

MIZPE MIDRAG

En-Gedi

Hever Caves

Hamme Mazor
Mineral Springs

HAR HOLED
510

Zeir
Anpin

THE DEAD SEA (MALCHUT)

At the end of the Jordan River, not far from Jericho, the Dead Sea stretches its salty waters. This is the lowest place in the world, where the fifth spiritual force, *Malchut*, manifests its quality.

Malchut is the future kingdom of Light, which will blossom forth from complete and utter egoism.

The water level in the Dead Sea is approximately 420 meters below sea level. Because of the high concentration of salt in its waters, life in it is virtually nonexistent. This is why it is called "The Dead Sea."

48

The Dead Sea is enclosed from east and west. On its western shore are the reddish brown bare rocky slopes of the Judea Desert, and past the eastern shore rise the Moav Mountains. Here and there, a lone settlement breaks the arid landscape of the desert.

The waters of the Dead Sea possess a unique quality—they are dense and heavy. After all, everything here contradicts the source from which the water springs.

There is a good reason why it is called "The Dead Sea," and there is a good reason why it has "embedded" itself so deeply in the ground.

Malchut symbolizes our world: On the one hand, it is lifeless in the spiritual sense, and on the other hand, it is craving to be revived. As odd as it may seem, *Malchut* is the final purpose, the destination to which all previous stages lead. Indeed, this lifeless and self-centered part must become the most vital, thriving, and the most similar to *Bina*—giving and loving.

THE PLACE WITH
THE STRONGEST
SPIRITUAL
INFLUENCE

The spiritual forces that affect our world drew Kabbalists, who study the superior reality, to a single point, much like electrons are drawn to the center of a force-field. They centered around the city of Safed, the highest and most northern of all the cities in the land of Israel. Here, Kabbalists found a place that coincided with the spiritual forces they had discovered.

Not far from Safed lies hidden a small cave called "The Idra Raba" (The Great Assembly). This is where Rabbi Shimon bar Yochai and his nine disciples wrote *The Book of Zohar*.

Rabbi Shimon bar Yochai was among the greatest Kabbalists of all time. He was the first to describe the spiritual world—the system that governs our world—in such great detail. In *The Book of Zohar*, he introduced the structure of reality, the gradual uncovering of the 125-stage spiritual reality, and the mechanism of spiritual ties that link us all together.

האדרא רבא

של

ר' שמעון בר יוחאי

ר' אלעזר

ר' אבא

ר' יהודה

ר' יוסי ברבי יעקוב

ר' יצחק

ר' חזקיה בר רב

ר' חייא

ר' יוסי

ר' ייסא

A cave is like a mother's womb. The climate inside the cave has healing powers, and a person is surrounded from all sides with the qualities of the earth: solid and soothing.

LIVING IN CAVES

People used to live in caves not because they didn't know how to build houses. They simply sensed the hidden force beneath the curves and arches. Today's high-rise buildings deprive us of that earth-born power.

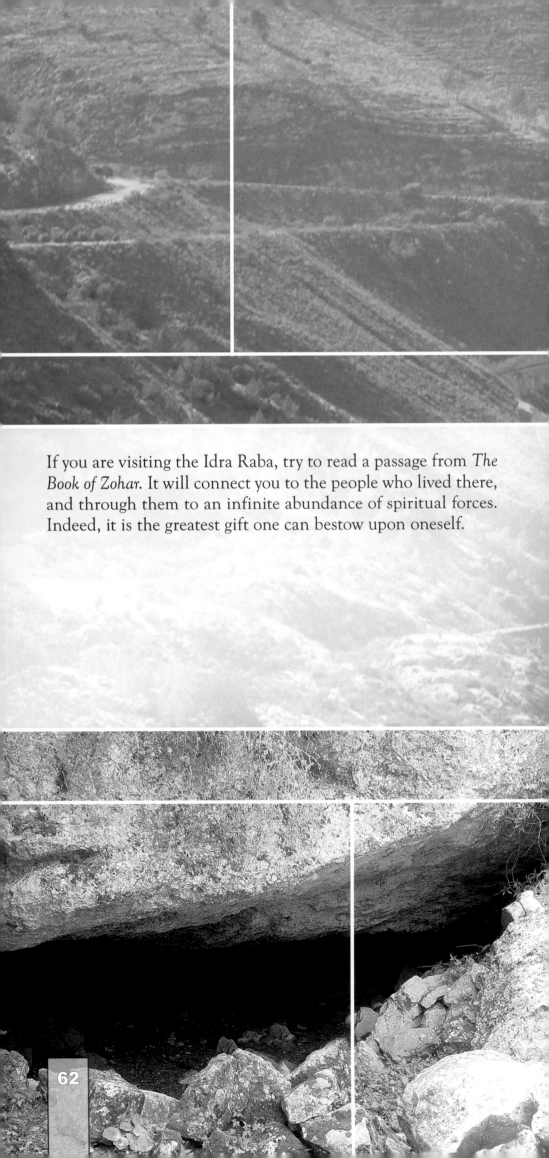

If you are visiting the Idra Raba, try to read a passage from *The Book of Zohar*. It will connect you to the people who lived there, and through them to an infinite abundance of spiritual forces. Indeed, it is the greatest gift one can bestow upon oneself.

CONTEMPORARY KABBALISTS

64

Rav Baruch Shalom Ashlag (1907-1991) was the last Kabbalist in a long line of Kabbalists that began with Abraham the Patriarch. Baruch Ashlag (known as Rabash) was the firstborn son and successor of the greatest Kabbalist in the 20th century, Rav Yehuda HaLevi Ashlag (1884-1954), author of the *Sulam* (Ladder) commentary on *The Book of Zohar*.

These two great Kabbalists "robed" the ancient wisdom in its contemporary "attire" and revealed it to the world.

The "pioneer" in disclosing Kabbalah was a great Kabbalist who lived in the 16th century. His name was Rabbi Isaac Luria Ashkenazi, and we know him as "the holy Ari." After he arrived in Safed, he adapted the Kabbalistic teaching and adjusted it to more modern thinking. The Ari marks a new stage in the history of humanity—the transition from the Middle Ages to the Renaissance, the era of revival.

MANY KABBALISTS LIVED IN SAFED
AND ITS SURROUNDINGS

Many of the authors of the Mishnah lived in Safed. Among the most notable of the sages was Rabbi Yonatan ben Uziel, who is buried in Amuka, not far from Safed. He was the greatest disciple of Old Hillel, who epitomized the whole Torah in the phrase, "That which you hate, do not do unto your friend."

Safed is a very special city that has long since been regarded as a spiritual center, "the capital of Kabbalah." Those who visit it sense the power of the place and "inhale" its unique atmosphere.

In his book, *A Grace unto Abraham* (Chapter 3, Item 13), Kabbalist Avraham ben Azulai said about the city: "Safed is suitable for a place in which to attain the depth of the Torah. There is no air as pure as the air of Safed in the whole of the land of Israel."

THE WORK OF THE KABBALISTS

A breathtaking view stretches out from the city of Safed—the Kinneret with its deep blue water sparkling under the warm sun. There is a famous story about the Ari, that once he took his prime disciple, Chaim Vital, to the Kinneret. As they were sailing in the lake, they reached a certain point in the water and the Ari halted the boat, took a handful of water in his palm, and gave some to his disciple to drink. This special place is called "Miriam's well."

Indeed, the story holds more than the superficial narrative; it carries a profound spiritual significance. Watering from Miriam's well symbolizes the spiritual act of a Kabbalist who is teaching his disciple about the quality of water—the quality of *Bina*—which is the quality of pure love and giving. Indeed, this is the entire work of Kabbalists: to teach us the meaning of true love.

WHERE ARE WE HEADED?

As we have said, the water flows down from the lush, mountainous area, *Keter*, down to the low and arid land, *Malchut*, to revive it and allow it to thrive. Just so, the influx of forces that are still hidden from us gushes into our world from the apex of reality. These lights revive us and bring us back to the origin of spiritual life.

The Holy Land lies in the very heart of all of these currents;
it is the center of the world. This is why it repeatedly finds
itself at the center of global events. It is a tiny patch of land,
barely visible on the map of the globe. And yet, this is where
everything begins and it is here to which everything returns.
Here, humankind's spiritual path remarkably intertwines with
hills and valleys, lakes and streams, towns and villages.

"The land of Israel resides in the middle of the world, and Jerusalem—in the middle of the land of Israel" (Midrash Tanhuma, Portion Kedoshim, Chapter 10).

ISRAEL
ROAD MAPS

SURVEY OF ISRAEL

LEGEND

SCALE 1:400,000
(1cm=4km)

10   5   0   10   20 km

Built-up area.....................................	
City, population 150,000 or more..........**HAIFA**	
Town, population less than 150,000............**LOD**	
Urban settlement, pop. 10,000 or more ⊙ GEDERA	
Rural settlement, pop. less than 10,000.⊙Deganya	
Locality.................................... ▪ Tel-Ḥay	
Antiquities..................................*Caesarea*	
Toll road.. ⑥	
Motorway, Interchange.............. ①	
Main road and tunnel................. ⑥⑤	
Regional road................................. ⑤⓪⑤	
Other road....................................	
All weather road, fuel station....	
Railway and station.........................	
Airport, airfield.................................	
Port...	
Perennial stream; watterfall.......	
Seasonal stream (wadi)................	
Canal...	
Lake, pond..	
Spring, well, water hole.....................	
Mineral spring..................................	
Spot height (meters)......................... •200	
Wood or forest.................................	

International boundary..................
Border Line according to the Israel-Jordan
Peace Treaty without precedence regarding
the status of the area to the west..
Zofar, Naharayim Zone Line..............
The Blue Line, Israel-Lebanon..........+ + + + +
(Established by the U.N. in the year 2000)

Lines of Disengagement of Forces, 1974:

Israeli Forward Line............................
Syrian Forward Line............................
Security Road......................................
Terminal...

Holy site:

Jewish.................	Christian.................		
Moslem..........	Druze.........	Bahai.........	
Church or monastery...........................			
Mosque...			
Ancient synagogue.............................			
Archaeological site, ruins..................			
Prehistoric site.................................			
Museum, visitor center..................			
Cave..			
Nature site, site of interest...............			
Observation tower.............................			
Observation point.............................			
Nature reserve and National park..................			
Field school....................................			
Youth hostel.....................................			
Picnic site..			
Excursion boat route, beach..................			
Marina or boating facilities..............			
Diving club......................................			
Skiing site..			

Wye Memorandum, Part 3, 20.3.2000

Area A - Palestinian responsibility for civil
affairs, internal security and public order.....

Area B - Palestinian responsibility for civil
affairs and public order of Palestinians.
Israeli responsibility for security of Israelis..

"Nature reserve"................................."Nature Reserve"

Note: Persons intending to enter areas defined
in the above mentioned memorandum are
advised to consult the appropriate authorities.

Coordinates:
Israel Grid in Blue
New Israel Grid in Red
This map is not an authority on boundaries

THE NUMBERS IN THE MAP MATCH THE PAGE
NUMBERS IN THE BOOK.

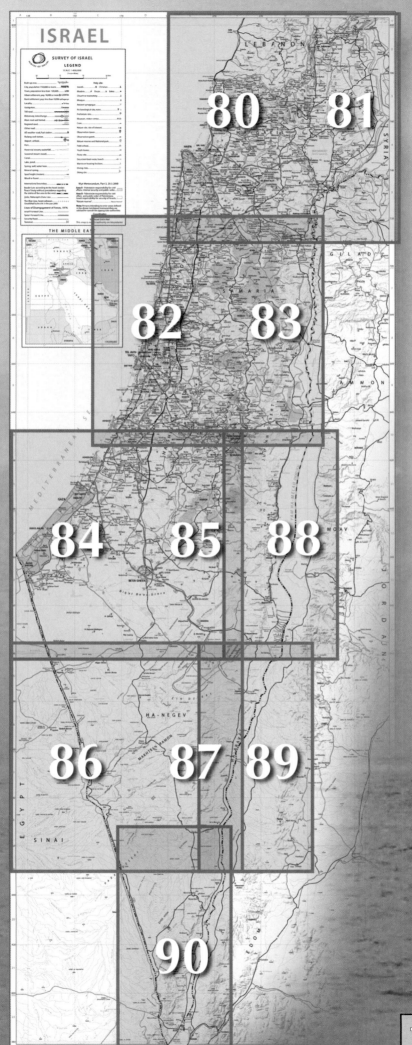

ISRAEL

THE MIDDLE EAS

80

81

82

83

84

85

88

86

87

89

90

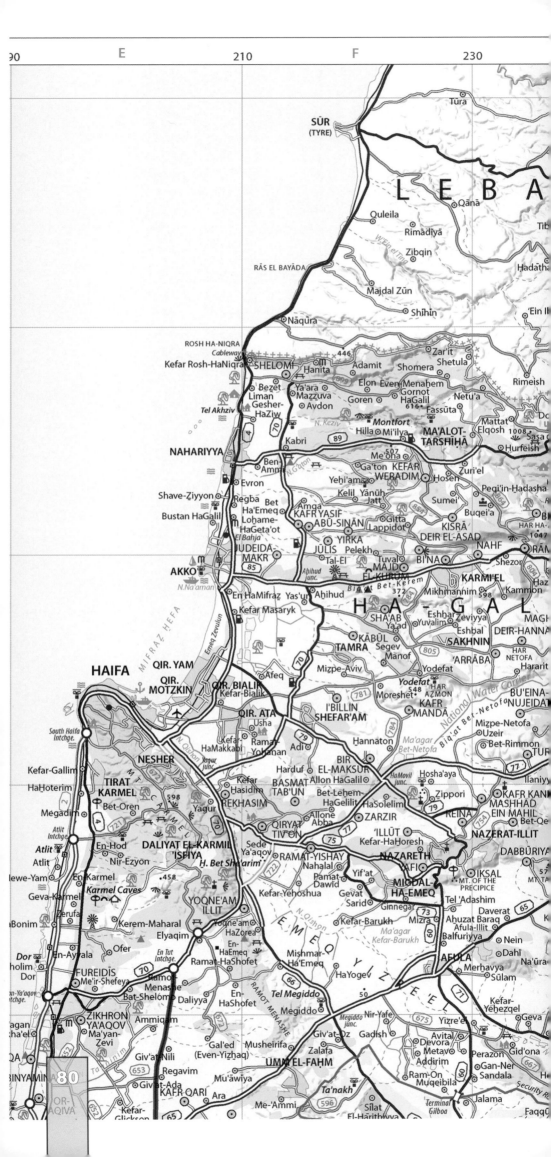

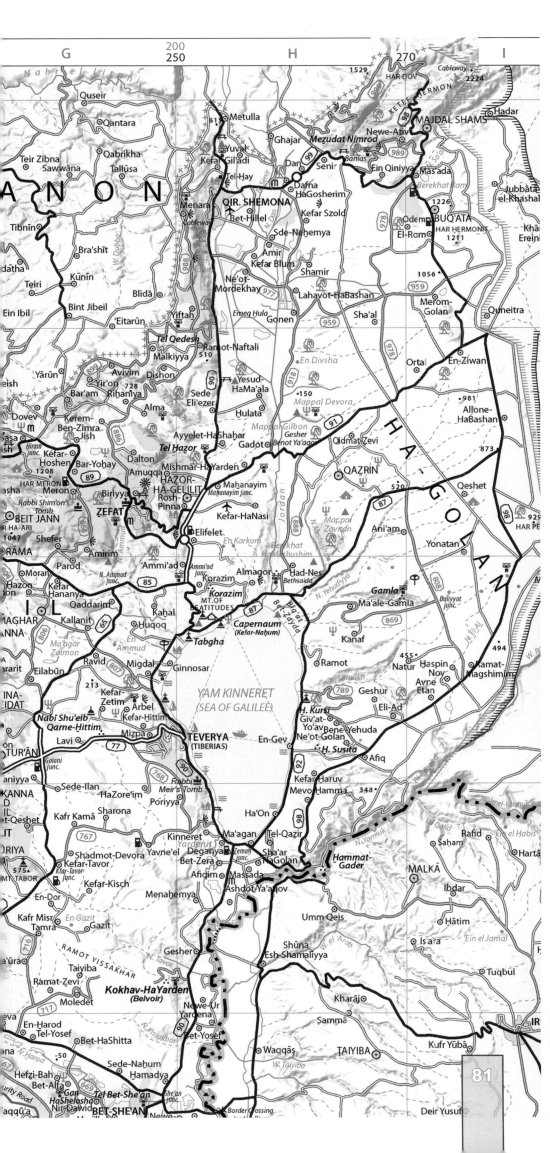

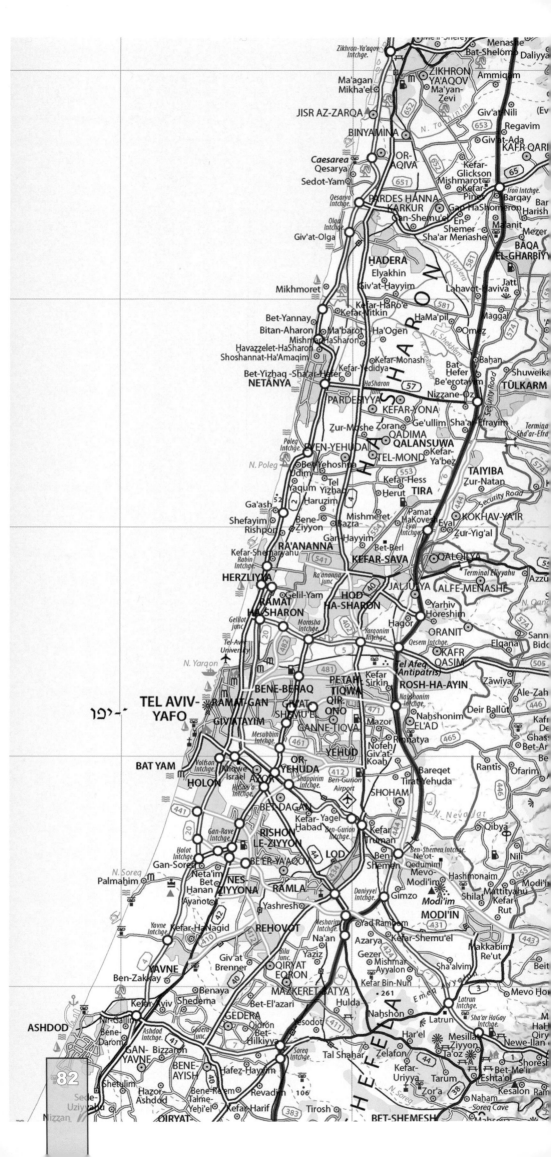

GAN
YAVN
Shetulim
Sede-
Uziyyahu
Nizzan
Giv'ati
Be'er-To
Kefar-W
Nizzanim
Mass
Yizh
Nir-Yisra'el
En-
ASHQELON
Kefar-Silver
Negba
Tel Ashqelon
Qomer
Yad-Natan
Bat-Hadar
Mash'en
Mavqi'im
Bet-Shiqma
Sede
Ge'a
Yo'av
Ziqim
Karmiyya
Kokhav-Mikha'el
Nogah
Ma'agar Shiqma
Talme-
Ma'agar
Yafe
Zohar
Yad Mordekhay
Zohar
Mordekhay
Ele-Sinay
junc.
(destroyed)
Netiv
Gevar'am
Helez
Dugit
HaAsara
N. Shiqma
(destroyed)
Erez
Sede-
Nisanit
Telamim
(destroyed)
Terminal
Or-HaNer
Beror Hayil
Erez
BEIT LAHIYA
SEDEROT
JABĀLĪYA
GAZA
Security Road
Nir-'Am
Gevim
Ru
Mefahasim
Dorot
Nezarim
Kefar-'Azza
Yakhini
(destroyed)
Nahal-Oz
Sa'ad
153
Nir-Moshe
Nir-Aqiva
Se
Terminal
25
Tequma
Zeru'a
Ze
Karni
Alumim
34
Qelahim
Eshbol
293
EL-BUREIJ
232
Shúva
Yoshivya
Be'eri
Tushiyya
Pa'ame-
DEIR EL-BALAH
NETIVOT
Talme Bilu
EL-MUGHĀZĪ
Shoqeda
Kefar-Darom
Tel Sera'
Sharsheret
(destroyed)
Ma'galim
Shibbolim
Tel Gamma
Re'im
Giv'olim
Tidhar
Melilot
131
Te'ashur
N. Gerar
Berosh
N. Pattish
Mishmar-
Banī
Kissufim
Rannen
Bitha
Suheila
242
Pattish
Maslul
KHAN YUNIS
Terminal
83•
Kissufim
En-HaShelosha
Peduyim
Gilat
Tifrah
Es
'ABASĀN
Nirim
Nahal Besor
234
Nir-Oz
241
Magen
En Besor
OFAQIM
241
Urim
Be'ar Manoah
173•
Security Road
Tel Sharuhen
RAFAH
Gevulot
Eh Sharuhen
Hazerim
(RAFIAH)
junc.
Terminal Sufa
En-HaBesor
Yesha
Border Crossing
Ammi'oz
222
Rafiah
Sufa
Zohar
Nir-Yizhaq
Mivtahim
240
Holit
Ohad
Talme
Peri-Gan
Eliyyahu
Kerem-
Sede-Nizzan
Shalom
Gevulot
Be'er Ze'elim
232
Sede-Avraham
Nahal Be'er-Sheva
Yated
Talme-Yosef
Ze'elim
•156
Be'er Asnat
Yevul
Deqel
10
B i q
GŌZ EL 'AYĀL
Holot Haluza
H. Haluza
GŌZ ES SAHAM
•154
Retamim
344•
Re
H. Rehovot (BaNegev)
Bi
84
Holot Agur
GIV'AT HAYIL
…aria
336
Holot Shunera
Ashalim

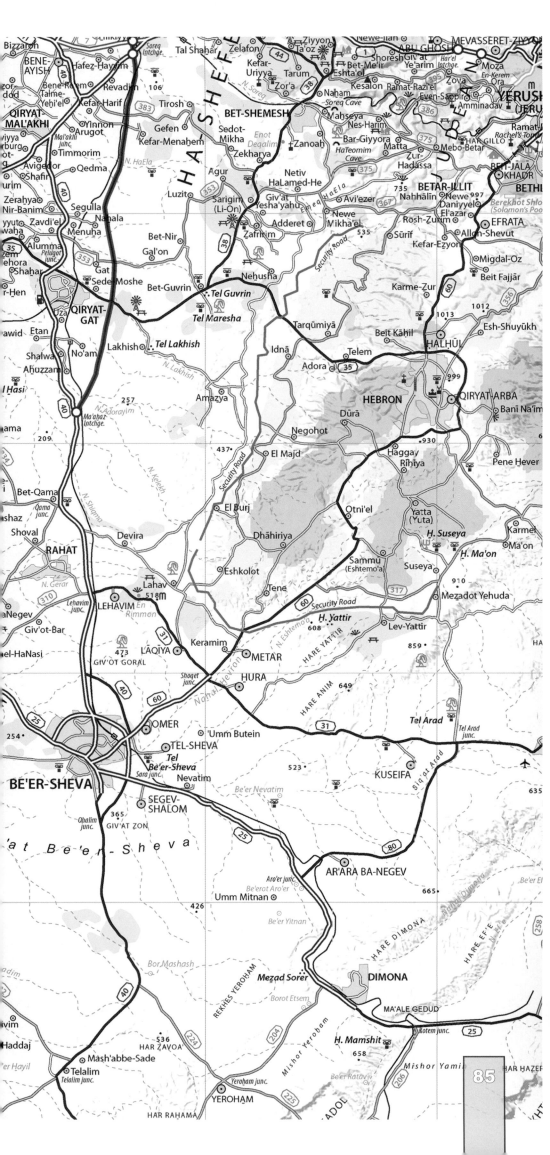

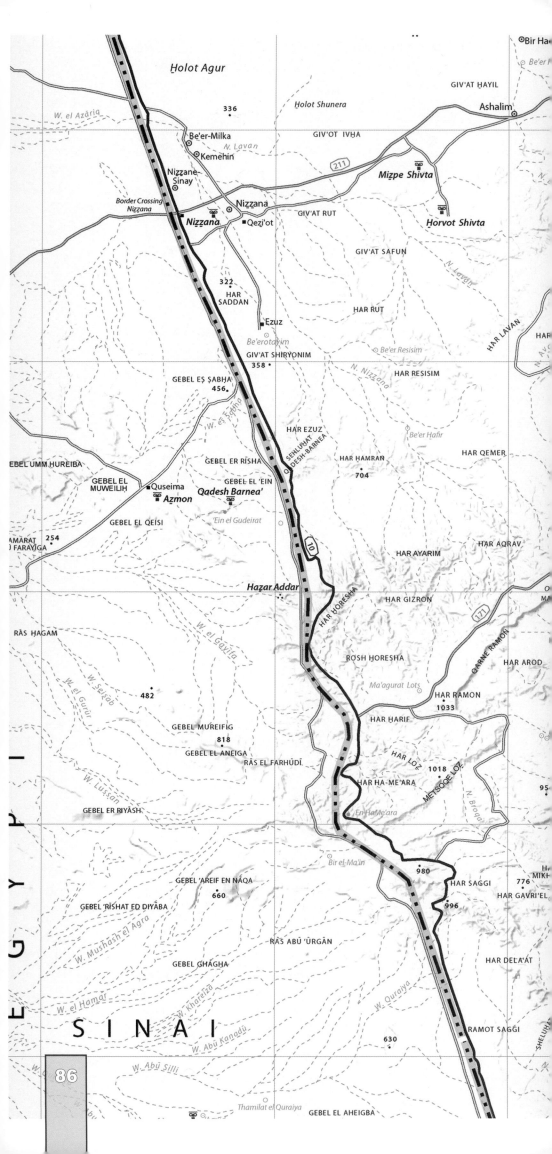

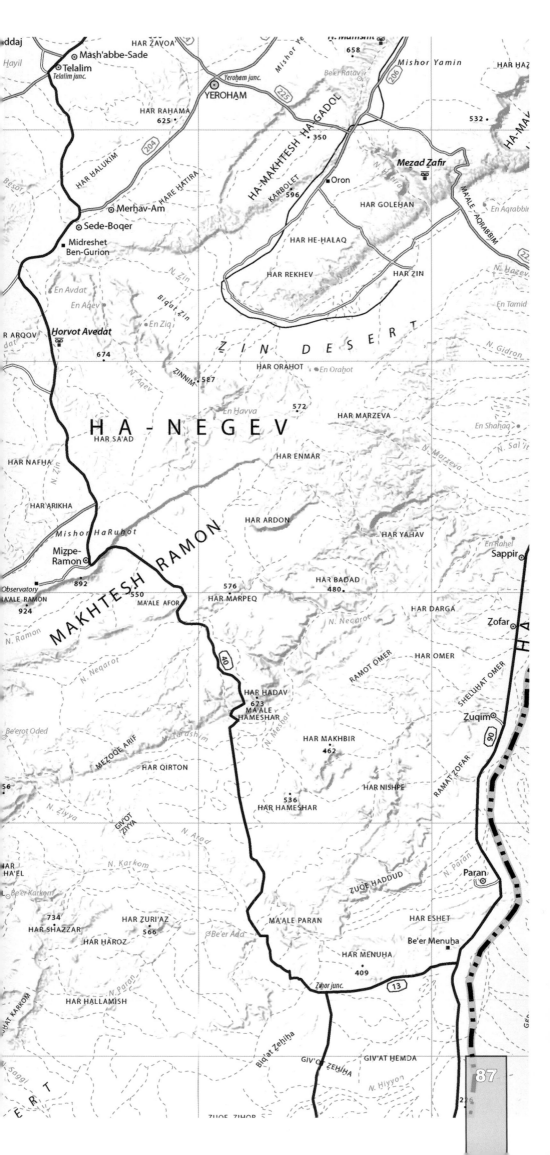

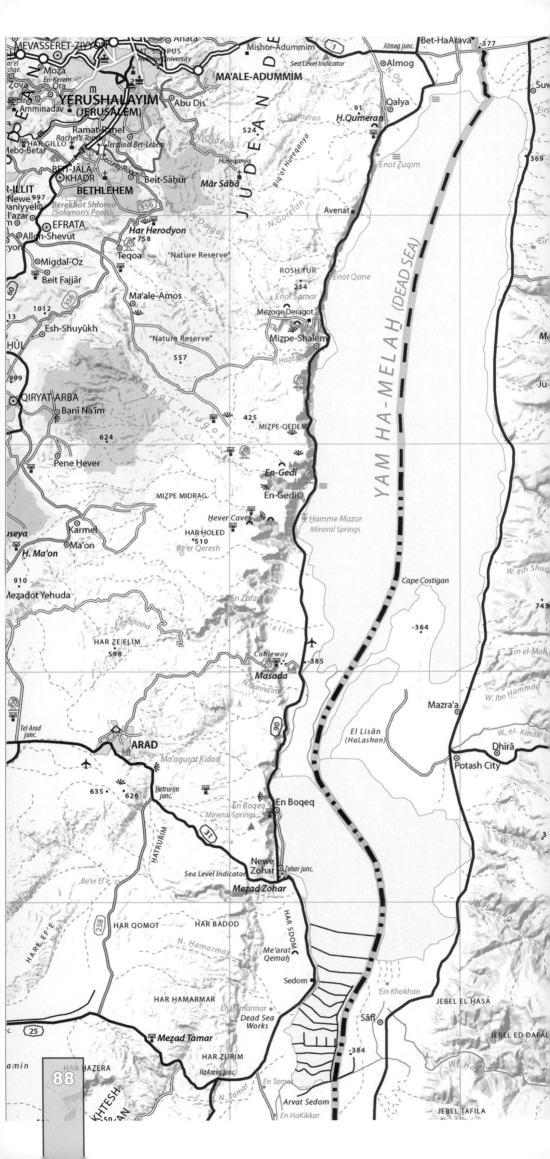

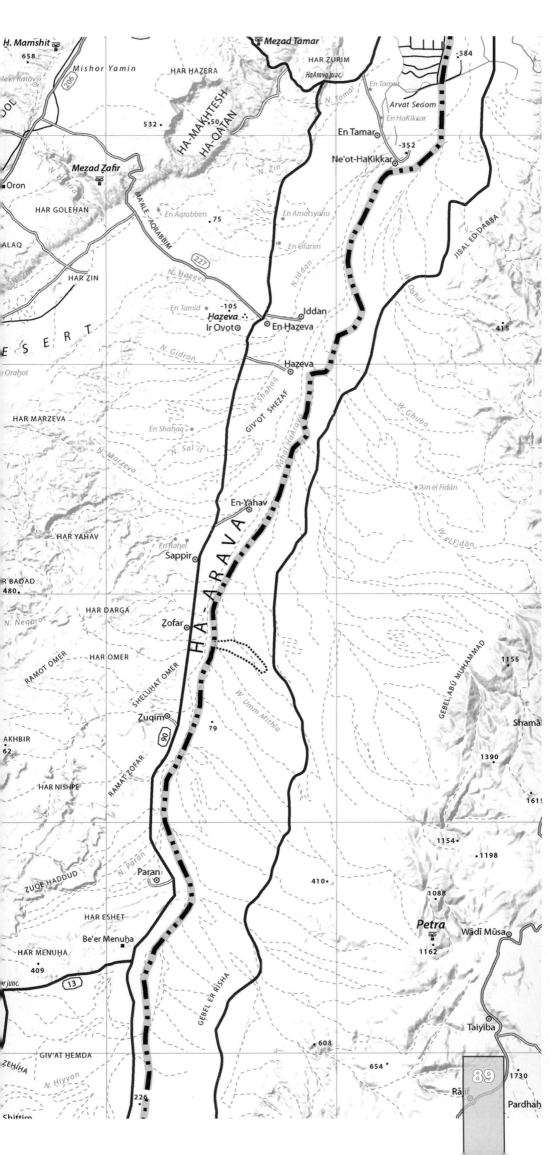

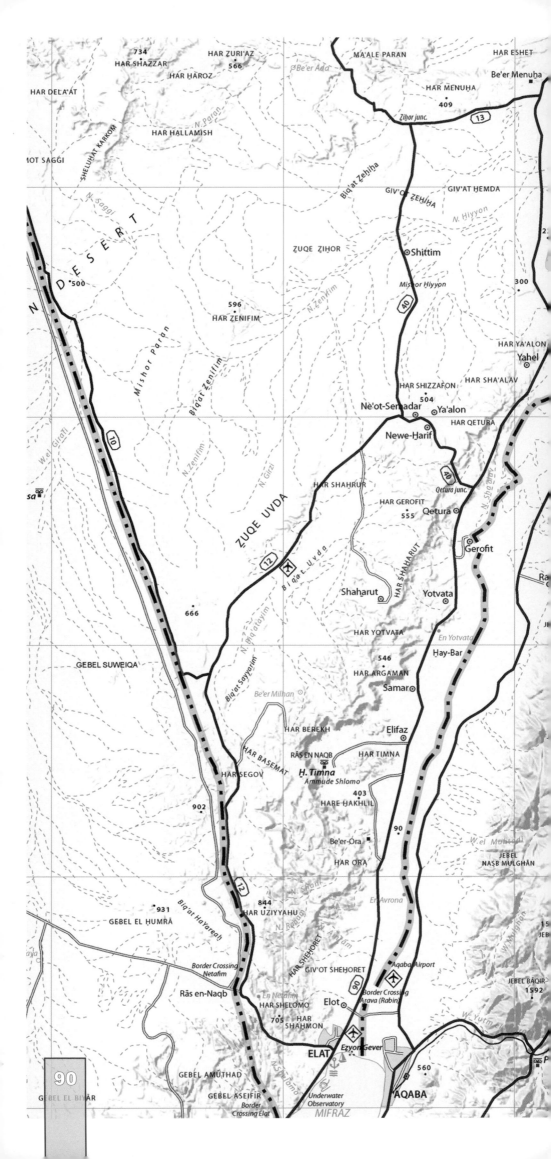

HAR SHAZZAR
734
HAR ZURI'AZ
566
HAR HAROZ
HAR DELA'AT
MA'ALE PARAN
HAR ESHET
Be'er Menuha
HAR MENUHA
409
Ø Be'er Ada
HAR HALLAMISH
N. Paran
Zihor junc.
13

SHELUHAT KARKOM
DESERT
N. Saggi
Biq'at Zehiha
GIV'OT ZEHIHA
GIV'AT HEMDA
N. Hiyyon
ZUQE ZIHOR
·500
Shittim
Mishor Hiyyon
300
40
596
HAR ZENIFIM
N. Zenifim
HAR YA'ALON
Mishor Paran
Yahel

W. el Girafi
Biq'at Zenifim
N. Zenifim
N. Zenifim
HAR SHIZZAFON
HAR SHA'ALAV
504
·sa
10
Ne'ot-Semadar
Ya'alon
HAR QETURA
N. Giraf
Newe-Harif
40
HAR SHAHRUR
Qetura junc.
N. Sha'alav
ZUQE UVDA
HAR GEROFIT
555
Qetura
Gerofit
12
Biq'at Uvda
HAR SHAHARUT
Ra
666
N. Biq'atayim
Shaharut
Yotvata
N. Biq'atayim
HAR YOTVATA
En Yotvata
JI

GEBEL SUWEIQA
546
Hay-Bar
HAR ARGAMAN
Biq'at Sayyarim
Samar
Be'er Milhan
HAR BEREKH
Elifaz
HAR BASEMAT
RAS EN NAQB
HAR TIMNA
HAR SEGOV
H. Timna
Ammude Shlomo
902
403
HARE HAKHLIL
W. el Muhtadi
Be'er-Ora
JEBEL
90
NASB MULGHAN
HAR ORA

12
931
844
En Avrona
N. Shani
GEBEL EL HUMRA
HAR UZIYYAHU
N. Roded
15
JEB

Aqaba Airport
JEBEL BAQIR
1592
Border Crossing
Netafim
HAR SHEHORET
GIV'OT SHEHORET
En Netafim
90
Border Crossing
Arava (Rabin)
Ras en-Naqb
HAR SHELOMO
Elot
W. Yutm
705
HAR
SHAHMON
ELAT
Ezyon Gever
560
P
GEBEL AMUTHAD
90
AQABA
GEBEL EL BIYAR
GEBEL ASEIFIR
Border
Crossing Elat
Underwater
Observatory
MIFRAZ

APPENDICES

What Is the Wisdom of Kabbalah?

The wisdom of Kabbalah is an age-old method that dates back to ancient Babylon. This method enables its students to understand where we come from and the reason why we live in this world. These answers can and must emerge in us while we are living here and now, and not in some other realm, detached from our reality.

Studying Kabbalah develops within us another sense, with which we can "penetrate" the "command center" of reality and understand how it runs, and how we can change our destiny for the best.

Indeed, the wisdom of Kabbalah is not a theoretical or abstract field of study, but rather a very practical one. Kabbalah doesn't engage in any mysticism and has nothing to do with charms, fortune-telling, or mascots such as red strings and so forth. It is also *not* intended for "unique individuals," but for anyone who seeks answers to the question about the meaning of life.

The wisdom of Kabbalah is the most natural and closest to our nature. Its aim is to help us understand ourselves, and come to know our nature. If we currently feel like a tiny part of a reality of which we have little or no control, Kabbalah comes to expand our range of "reception" so we may discover the entirety of the rich and magnificent reality we live in, and to teach us how to control it.

While studying, we gradually discover what we need to do to experience a better reality. We slowly learn to understand our desires and emotions, and how we can funnel them in the right direction. In short, Kabbalah is a method for discovering the superior force that governs our lives.

To study Kabbalah, we need not perform any physical actions, rituals, or chants. All the transformations and research are done within, in a part that is hidden from sight. This is why Kabbalah is called "the wisdom of the hidden."

A Brief History of Kabbalah

According to the wisdom of Kabbalah, at the core of human nature lies the desire to enjoy. This desire is embedded in all humans and demands of us to do *everything* to satisfy the demand for pleasure, even at the expense of others. In fact, everything we do, from the smallest and simplest act to the most complicated and demanding is intended only to enhance our sensation of pleasure or diminish the sensation of pain.

Throughout history, the human desire for pleasure (a.k.a. ego) has set the wheels of human development in motion, leading it to grand achievements. Man's growing desires are causing us to run from pleasure to pleasure, forever seeking new ways of gratification.

The five stages of development of desire have yielded the development of hierarchical systems that have transformed the socioeconomic structure of society, in many cases becoming the primary cause of wars and revolutions that have scarred the memory of humanity all through history.

The desire for knowledge and erudition that began to develop following the desires for wealth, power, and domination has prompted us to develop science, education systems, and culture, and has left its mark on us since the Renaissance through the present.

Succinctly, the history of humanity can be paralleled with the evolution of the desire to enjoy, the ego. Emerging from this concept, Kabbalists tend to divide the history of humanity into five focal points, in each of which a "leap" occurred in the evolution of human egoism. Below is a brief description of the five.

Abraham—the First Mark

The first of the five milestones in the evolution of the human ego was laid down approximately 4,000 years ago in ancient Babylon, today's Iraq.

In those days, life was rather peaceful in Babylon. The residents sensed natural affinity to one another and the whole city lived as one big family. But then the ego began to burst and matters took a sudden shift. Suddenly, the simple life of a herdsman or the residence of a cave seemed dull and unsatisfying. The Babylonians began to want more, much more.

Soon, agriculture became far more developed, the foundations of trade, and the use of currency and taxation were established. Alongside that, methods of governance and management evolved, establishing law and order, which we now call "bureaucracy."

The social transformation yielded classes and social statuses. The ego that was prompting the Babylonians to develop was also making them more self-centered, and thus separated them like a knife.

The famous Tower of Babel is the epitome of that self-centered drive. The Babylonians thought that they could reach the heaven and even rule Nature, the upper force. Yet, within a short period of time the ego has become so overblown that they could no longer understand each other and the single language that they spoke until that time had splintered into the myriad languages and dialects that exist today.

Abraham, who was an idol-worshipper like the rest of his compatriots, saw the process in its very onset. However, unlike his contemporaries he refused to succumb to the circumstances and decided to study the reasons for shift in depth. His research of reality had led him to know his Maker. And knowing the upper force made him realize two pivotal points:

1. The comprehensive force that operates reality and governs it is a force of pure love and giving. Its purpose is to lead all the people in the world to equality and harmony with it. Also, disharmony with that force yields negative effects that find their expressions in sufferings of all sorts.

2. The heightening ego is in contrast with that force of love and giving, hence it is destined to lead the Babylonians into ruin.

Through the knowledge of the spiritual world that he acquired, Abraham developed and systematic method for transcending the ego. Abraham tried to explain that the ego was not intended to separate us. On the contrary, it is meant to make us unite in a truer and stronger bond, on top of it. Its outburst is an opportunity for a positive shift, if we are wise enough to unite in love of others on top of the erupting ego, by balancing with the upper forces. Thus, he explained, we could rise to a higher level of existence and thrive.

Alas, only few of the Babylonians heeded the advice of the great sage. Those few realized the method on themselves and achieved a state of love of others among them. In time, they became what we now call "the people of Israel."

Moses—Escaping the Rule of Egoism

The golden age of Egypt marks a new stage in the heightening of human egoism. In those days, fierce battles among empires and enslavement of entire nations were the norm. The people of Israel, which went down to Egypt to buy food because of the drought in the land of Israel, soon found a new home in Egypt's fertile land of Goshen.

But Egypt represents the growing ego in humanity of those days, and gradually, the welcome guests became enslaved by the Egyptians. To deliver the people from enslavement (both internal enslavement to the ego, and external enslavement to the Egyptians), a strong leader was required, to lead the people to a higher state of being. And indeed, Moses, the next great sage appeared—Moses.

Moses faced Pharaoh and struggled with him for the spiritual future of the people of Israel. But this was not enough. Delivering the people from Egypt required complete unification of the people. For this purpose, Moses took the method that Abraham first discovered, and adapted it to the new level of egoism. With it, he united the people and brought them out of Egypt. The "guide" he wrote for deliverance from egoism is now known as "The Torah," the "Five Books of Moses."

Throughout ancient history, love of others has been the key to the success of the people of Israel. As long as it maintained the bonding and love among its members, it maintained its spiritual and corporeal integrity. This culminated in the days of the united kingdom of Israel and the building of the First Temple.

But then the ego erupted once again and the unity was interrupted when a group of Israelites became self-centered. The results soon followed and the spiritual divide led to corporeal destruction. The First Temple was ruined and the people were exiled into Babylon once more. But when the people united, they were given the land once more and built the Second Temple.

Yet, the evolution of the ego did not pause in its growth. It erupted once again with an even deeper rift, which engulfed the entire nation. The known maxim, "Love your neighbor as yourself," has turned into unfounded hatred, and the spiritual decline was so intense that it led to the ruin of the Second Temple.

Rabbi Shimon bar Yochai and the Hidden Book of Zohar

To restore the spiritual state that existed at the time of the Temples, the next great Kabbalist arose—Rabbi Shimon bar Yochai. For 13 years! Rabbi Shimon sat with his son, Rabbi Elazar, in a little cave in Peki'in, a small village in the Galilee. They were preparing themselves for the writing of the book that was to change the course of history. When they felt that the time was ripe, they emerged from the cave, gathered 8 more Kabbalists, and all 10 settled in another cave, overlooking the mountainous view of the city of Safed.

And while bloodshed and wars were the everyday reality of the time, these 10 sages wrote a book about eternity and everlasting love, known as *The Book of Zohar*.

The Book of Zohar is the seminal book of Kabbalah. And yet, soon after they wrote it, its authors concealed it, since the world was not ready for it to become publicly known.

"The book," said Rabbi Shimon, "Will appear only in a generation when people have given up on the egoistic route and have begun to seek the meaning of life. Its role will be to end the era of spiritual darkness, the exile." Indeed, from that time, in the 2nd century C.E., until the 16th century, the wisdom of Kabbalah remained a secret teaching and was developed behind closed doors, waiting for its turn to shine.

But in the 16th century, a new dawn was shining. In humanity, it was the height of the Renaissance. In Kabbalah, the next great Kabbalist appeared—Rabbi Isaac Luria Ashkenazi, the holy Ari.

The Holy Ari—a New Era

The 16th century was the start of an unprecedented shift in history. Everything began to accelerate—scientific and industrial revolutions unfolded, rebellions and civil wars struck the world over, and radical shifts took place between the 16th and 19th centuries. To prevent the horrible suffering and promote humanity toward spirituality, a special soul appeared in our world: the holy Ari. His role was quite similar to that of his predecessors—to adapt the wisdom of Kabbalah to the new emerging era.

It is not without merit that the Ari symbolizes the beginning of redemption from the last exile. After many centuries of Kabbalah being hidden by the Kabbalists themselves, it was now time to disclose it to the world.

The arrival of the Ari in Safed was the start of a fascinating historic process. During the 18 months of the Ari's staying in Safed, he turned the wisdom of Kabbalah from a method suitable for a chosen few, into a method for all of humanity.

And yet, in those days only a few felt the need to put the Ari's method into serious practice. Apparently, humanity needed further ripening and developing.

Baal HaSulam—Sharing the Wisdom of Kabbalah with the World

The 20th century was the most intense and dense century in history. It seems as though time became "condensed" during it. At the start of the century, railroads were the apex of technology. But by 1969, humankind had already made the "giant step" of reaching the moon. During that century, we have become a global village, wired to the Internet and too attached to our cellphones. We also killed more than 120 million people in two world wars, a concept that never existed prior to the 20th century.

At the start of the 21st century, humanity is encountering a new phenomenon that seems to affect all realms of life: emptiness. The global crisis we are witnessing today announces the arrival of a new era, a new need that is percolating to the surface. It is a sign that now is the time when every person in the world can approach the genuine sources of Kabbalah and draw from them the needed guidance for navigating in a world of new directions.

And as with any new era, a special Kabbalist appeared in our world to map out the path to our success. His name was Rav Yehuda Ashlag, also known as Baal HaSulam (Owner of the Ladder) for his *Sulam* (Ladder) commentary on *The Book of Zohar*.

In addition to his *Sulam* commentary, Baal HaSulam wrote an extensive commentary on the writings of the Ari, known as *The Study of the Ten Sefirot*, where he explained the Kabbalistic concepts and made them approachable to the current generation.

Baal HaSulam also wrote numerous essays, books, published a paper, met with politicians and traveled to many places only to explain the wisdom of Kabbalah. At the time, His ideas sounded revolutionary. But today we see that they are not only applicable, but necessary for the survival of the human race on the planet.

Indeed, this great man led a spiritual revolution whose fruits are only now becoming evident. Thanks to him, the circle has been completed and the books of Kabbalah that were hidden for centuries are becoming mainstream, a welcome change in a world thirsty for guidance. Today the world is ready, and The *Book of Zohar* is appearing, along with the explanation that makes it clear to every person whose heart desires to perceive it.

About Bnei Baruch

Bnei Baruch is an international group of Kabbalists who share the wisdom of Kabbalah with the entire world. The study materials (in over 30 languages) are authentic Kabbalah texts that were passed down from generation to generation.

The essence of the message disseminated by Bnei Baruch is universal: unity of the people, unity of nations and love of man.

For millennia, Kabbalists have been teaching that love of man should be the foundation of all human relations. This love prevailed in the days of Abraham, Moses, and the group of Kabbalists that they established. If we make room for these seasoned, yet contemporary values, we will discover that we possess the power to put differences aside and unite.

The wisdom of Kabbalah, hidden for millennia, has been waiting for the time when we would be sufficiently developed and ready to implement its message. Now, it is emerging as a solution that can unite diverse factions everywhere, enabling us, as individuals and as a society, to meet today's challenges.

How To Contact Bnei Baruch

1057 Steeles Avenue West, Suite 532
Toronto, ON, M2R 3X1
Canada

Bnei Baruch USA,
2009 85th street, #51,
Brooklyn, New York, 11214
USA

E-mail: info@kabbalah.info
Web site: www.kabbalah.info

Toll free in USA and Canada:
1-866-LAITMAN
Fax: 1-905 886 9697

Recommended Books

A Guide to the Hidden Wisdom of Kabbalah

A Guide to the Hidden Wisdom of Kabbalah is a light and reader-friendly guide to beginners in Kabbalah, covering everything from the history of Kabbalah to how this wisdom can help resolve the world crisis.

The book is set up in three parts: Part 1 covers the history, facts, and fallacies about Kabbalah, and introduces its key concepts. Part 2 tells you all about the spiritual worlds and other neat stuff like the meaning of letters and the power of music. Part 3 covers the implementation of Kabbalah at a time of world crisis.

Kabbalah Revealed:
A Guide to a More Peaceful Life

This is the most clearly written, reader-friendly guide to making sense of the surrounding world. Each of its six chapters focuses on a different aspect of the wisdom of Kabbalah, illuminating its teachings and explaining them using various examples from our day-to-day lives.

The first three chapters in Kabbalah Revealed explain why the world is in a state of crisis, how our growing desires promote progress as well as alienation, and why the biggest deterrent to achieving positive change is rooted in our own spirits. Chapters Four through Six offer a prescription for positive change. In these chapters, we learn how we can use our spirits to build a personally peaceful life in harmony with all of Creation.

Wondrous Wisdom

This book offers an initial course on Kabbalah. Like all the books presented here, Wondrous Wisdom is based solely on authentic teachings passed down from Kabbalist teacher to student over thousands of years. At the heart of the book is a sequence of lessons revealing the nature of Kabbalah's wisdom and explaining how to attain it. For every person questioning "Who am I really?" and "Why am I on this planet?" this book is a must.

Awakening to Kabbalah:
The Guiding Light of Spiritual Fulfillment

A distinctive, personal, and awe-filled introduction to an ancient wisdom tradition. In this book, Rav Laitman offers a deeper understanding of the fundamental teachings of Kabbalah, and how you can use its wisdom to clarify your relationship with others and the world around you.

Using language both scientific and poetic, he probes the most profound questions of spirituality and existence. This provocative, unique guide will inspire and invigorate you to see beyond the world as it is and the limitations of your everyday life, become closer to the Creator, and reach new depths of the soul.

Kabbalah for Beginners

Kabbalah for Beginners is a book for all those seeking answers to life's essential questions. We all want to know why we are here, why there is pain, and how we can make life more enjoyable. The four parts of this book provide us with reliable answers to these questions, as well as clear explanations of the gist of Kabbalah and its practical implementations.

Part One discusses the discovery of the wisdom of Kabbalah, and how it was developed, and finally concealed until our time. Part Two introduces the gist of the wisdom of Kabbalah, using ten easy drawings to help us understand the structure of the spiritual worlds, and how they relate to our world. Part Three reveals Kabbalistic concepts that are largely unknown to the public, and Part Four elaborates on practical means you and I can take, to make our lives better and more enjoyable for us and for our children.

The Book of Zohar:
annotations to the Ashlag commentary

The Book of Zohar (The Book of Radiance) is an age-old source of wisdom and the basis for all Kabbalistic literature. Since its appearance nearly 2,000 years ago, it has been the primary, and often only, source used by Kabbalists.

For centuries, Kabbalah was hidden from the public, which was deemed not yet ready to receive it. However, our generation has been designated by Kabbalists as the first generation that is ready to grasp the concepts in The Zohar. Now we can put these principles into practice in our lives.

Written in a unique and metaphorical language, The Book of Zohar enriches our understanding of reality and widens our worldview. Although the text deals with one subject only—how to relate to the Creator—it approaches it from different angles. This allows each of us to find the particular phrase or word that will carry us into the depths of this profound and timeless wisdom.

The Point in the Heart:
A Source of Delight for My Soul

The Point in the Heart; a Source of Delight for My Soul is a unique collection of excerpts from a man whose wisdom has earned him devoted students in North America and the world over. Michael Laitman is a scientist, a Kabbalist, and a great thinker who presents ancient wisdom in a compelling style.

This book does not profess to teach Kabbalah, but rather gently introduces ideas from the teaching. The Point in the Heart is a window to a new perception. As the author himself testifies to the wisdom of Kabbalah, "It is a science of emotion, a science of pleasure. You are welcome to open and to taste."

Attaining the Worlds Beyond

From the introduction to Attaining the Worlds Beyond: "...Not feeling well on the Jewish New Year's Eve of September 1991, my teacher called me to his bedside and handed me his notebook, saying, 'Take it and learn from it.' The following morning, he perished in my arms, leaving me and many of his other disciples without guidance in this world.

"He used to say, 'I want to teach you to turn to the Creator, rather than to me, because He is the only strength, the only Source of all that exists, the only one who can really help you, and He awaits your prayers for help. When you seek help in your search for freedom from the bondage of this world, help in elevating yourself above this world, help in finding the self, and help in determining your purpose in life, you must turn to the Creator, who sends you all those aspirations in order to compel you to turn to Him.'"

Attaining the Worlds Beyond holds within it the content of that notebook, as well as other inspiring texts. This book reaches out to all those seekers who want to find a logical, reliable way to understand the world's phenomena. This fascinating introduction to the wisdom of Kabbalah will enlighten the mind, invigorate the heart, and move readers to the depths of their souls.

Children of Tomorrow:
Guidelines for Raising Happy Children in the 21st Century

Children of Tomorrow is a new beginning for you and your children. Imagine being able to hit the reboot button and get it right this time. No hassle, no stress, and best of all—no guessing.

The big revelation is that raising kids is all about games and play, relating to them as small grownups, and making all major decisions together. You will be surprised to discover how teaching kids about positive things like friendship and caring for others automatically spills into other areas of our lives through the day.

Open any page and you will find thought-provoking quotes about every aspect of children's lives: parent-children relations, friendships and conflicts, and a clear picture of how schools should be designed and function. This book offers a fresh perspective on how to raise our children, with the goal being the happiness of all children everywhere.

The Wise Heart:
Tales and allegories by three contemporary sages

"Our inner work is to tune our hearts and our senses to perceive the spiritual world," says Michael Laitman in the poem Spiritual Wave. The Wise Heart is a lovingly crafted anthology comprised of tales and allegories by Kabbalist Dr. Michael Laitman, his mentor, Rav Baruch Ashlag (Rabash), and Rabash's father and mentor, Rav Yehuda Ashlag, author of the acclaimed Sulam (Ladder) commentary on The Book of Zohar.

Kabbalah students and enthusiasts in Kabbalah often wonder what the spiritual world actually feels like to a Kabbalist. The allegories in this delicate compilation provide a glimpse into those feelings.

The poems herein are excerpts from letters and lessons given by these three spiritual giants to their students through the years. They offer surprising and often amusing depictions of human nature, with a loving and tender touch that is truly unique to Kabbalists. Indeed, The Wise Heart is a gift of wisdom and delight for any wisdom seeking heart.

Shamati (I Heard)

Rav Michael Laitman's words on the book: Among all the texts and notes that were used by my teacher, Rav Baruch Shalom Halevi Ashlag (the Rabash), there was one special notebook he always carried. This notebook contained the transcripts of his conversations with his father, Rav Yehuda Leib Halevi Ashlag (Baal HaSulam), author of the Sulam (Ladder) commentary on The Book of Zohar, The Study of the Ten Sefirot (a commentary on the texts of the Kabbalist, Ari), and of many other works on Kabbalah.

Not feeling well on the Jewish New Year's Eve of September 1991, the Rabash summoned me to his bedside and handed me a notebook, whose cover contained only one word, Shamati (I Heard). As he handed the notebook, he said, "Take it and learn from it." The following morning, my teacher perished in my arms, leaving me and many of his other disciples without guidance in this world.

Committed to Rabash's legacy to disseminate the wisdom of Kabbalah, I published the notebook just as it was written, thus retaining the text's transforming powers. Among all the books of Kabbalah, Shamati is a unique and compelling creation.

Children's Books

The Baobab that Opened Its Heart:
and Other Nature Tales for Children

The Baobab that Opened Its Heart is a collection of stories for children, but not just for them. The stories in this collection were written with the love of nature, of people, and specifically with children in mind. They all share the desire to tell nature's tale of unity, connectedness, and love.

Kabbalah teaches that love is nature's guiding force, the reason for creation. The stories in this book convey it in the unique way that Kabbalah engenders in its students. The variety of authors and diversity of styles allows each reader to find the story that they like most.

Miracles Can Happen:
Tales for children, but not only...

"Miracles Can Happen," Princes Peony," and "Mary and the Paints" are only three of ten beautiful stories for children ages 3-10. Written especially for children, these short tales convey a single message of love, unity, and care for all beings. The unique illustrations were carefully crafted to contribute to the overall message of the book, and a child who's heard or read any story in this collection is guaranteed to go to sleep smiling.

Together Forever:
The story about the magician who didn't want to be alone

On the surface, Together Forever is a children's story. But like all good children's stories, it transcends boundaries of age, culture, and upbringing.

In Together Forever, the author tells us that if we are patient and endure the trials we encounter along our life's path, we will become stronger, braver, and wiser. Instead of growing weaker, we will learn to create our own magic and our own wonders as only a magician can.

In this warm, tender tale, Michael Laitman shares with children and parents alike some of the gems and charms of the spiritual world. The wisdom of Kabbalah is filled with spellbinding stories. Together Forever is yet another gift from this ageless source of wisdom, whose lessons make our lives richer, easier, and far more fulfilling.